"Art is a platform for experience, not a lesson"
Klaus Kertess

NIGHTWALKING
voices from Kent State

Sandra Perlman

Franklin Mills Press
Kent Ohio

Copyright © 1995 By Sandra Perlman

Nightwalking is published by Franklin Mills Press,
P.O. Box 906, Kent, OH 44240

All rights reserved. Except for brief passages quoted in newspaper, magazines, radio, or television reviews, no part of this book may be reproduced in any form or by any means, electronic or mechanical, including photocopying or recording, or by an information storage and retrieval system, without permission in writing from the publisher.

Professionals and amateurs are hereby warned that this material, being fully protected under the Copyright Laws of the United States of America and all other countries of the Berne and Universal Copyright Conventions, is subject to royalty. All rights, including, but not limited to, professional, amateur, recording, motion picture, recitation, lecturing, public reading, radio and television broadcasting, and the rights of translation into foreign languages are expressly reserved. Particular emphasis is placed on the question of readings and all uses of this play by educational institutions, permission for which must be secured from the author's representative, Franklin Mills Press, P.O. Box 906, Kent, Ohio 44240, (216) 673-8632 Fax (216) 677-2488.

Perlman, Sandra
    Nightwalking (voices from Kent State)

ISBN 1-885663-01-3

Book design and composition by the Franklin Mills Press

First Edition, April 1995

Production History

I am grateful to those actors, directors and designers who have worked with me to transform *Nightwalking* from dreams to text to the stage.

The World Premiere of *Nightwalking* was presented in Chicago by Terrapin Theatre on April 20, 1995 at the Organic Theater Greenhouse. It was directed by Jenifer (Gwenne) Weber. Sets and lighting were designed by Daniel Michael Frazier with props and costumes by Crystal O'Mara. Sound was designed by Christopher Walz and Tami Zimmerman assisted with stage movement. Michelle Landes was the Stage Manager. Pam Dickler and Frank Stilwagner were Producers. The cast was as follows:

MARGOT	Beverly Coscarelli
FRANK WOODSON	Michael Sobczak
CATHERINE WOODSON	Michelle Kalisiak
RICHARD	James Eldrenkamp
SHANNON	Susan Shimer
KENT	Robert Teverbaugh
MICHAEL WOODSON	Matthew Walker
ANONYMOUS WOMAN	Gail Biek
GUARDSMAN	Rick Kay

PLAYWRIGHT'S NOTES

I moved to Kent, Ohio in 1969, the same week Neil Armstrong walked on the moon. In retrospect, it was easier to focus our attention so far away since the unfamiliar terrain was increasingly at home. In many families, there was a growing sense of alienation between parents and their children. Conceived in the flush of America's post World War II victory and economic success, life was changing, and sons and daughters were often viewed as part of a new world that was too loud, too rude and too unpredictable. Plant closings, political assassination, nuclear weapons, urban riots, as well as more and more vocal protests against the war in Vietnam seemed to be taking us to a place as foreign as that faraway moon. And then there was always - sex, drugs and rock 'n roll.

On Sunday May 3rd, my husband and I walked around the Kent campus; the next day, when the Guard opened fire, my husband was standing on the other side of the hill and I was teaching in a high school in Akron. More observer than participant, I have tried to understand the forces that culminated in those 13 seconds of gunfire and connect them back to my own personal experiences.

For many people in the town, on the campus, and throughout this country, the shootings at Kent came to symbolize either a beginning - or an end. But no matter how one felt about the tragedy, it could not be ignored.

Though I tried to deal with those events more obliquely in previous plays, May 4th would surface directly in *Cliff Diving*, my play about twenty years in the life of a northeast Ohio family named Woodson. In 1990 during the 20th anniversary of the shootings, I created an oral history project so that ordinary people might leave behind their own memories of those turbulent times and how it had resonated in their own lives. I initially hoped these stories would act as a vehicle for the healing of those who told them as well as my own need to find closure. I also hoped it would add another dimension to the research that could be used to continue the study of those days. And in some innocent way, I think I still expected some mysterious person to appear who would provide the missing links to how this tragedy had ever happened.

In the days that followed, I heard many stories that added to my own memories. Somehow, with some of these new perspectives, I lost the need to find one single answer. Like Rashomon, there were simply too many versions of the same reality. The events were no longer a mystery play that needed to be solved. Looking again at all the players involved during those times of what I saw as our second civil war, as well as the insistence on our litany of innocence - "how could there have been loaded guns" - the dramatic conclusion that day seemed less mysterious and more inevitable than ever.

In 1993 I joined a group of playwrights at The Cleveland Play House and over that winter we were to bring in a new piece that we were writing. The voices and characters who had coalesced into the cast of my play suddenly demanded to be heard. So I wrote them down. And in the spirit of storytelling - I am now passing them on to you. None of these stories is pure fact, though none is purely fiction.

ACKNOWLEDGMENTS

I am grateful to The Cleveland Play House playwrights who gave me my first constructive criticism after the first reading of *Nightwalking* in the spring of 1994. Those suggestions encouraged me to include more historical markers in this draft which has also benefited from trying to answer Michael Burnham's endless questions. Thanks to Calvin McClinton who became the Godfather of its first two productions. Jenifer (Gwenne) Weber and Terrapin Theatre for their faith in the script, and Mitchel DeVol for planning to direct a production at Kent State this May. My gratitude to Linda Eisenstein who helped me edit this book, and Angela Johnson who helped me keep the faith. Special thanks to Nancy Birk and the KSU Special Collections who supported the original Oral History Project, and all of those who chose to come forward and leave their stories. It will matter.

Finally, I continue to be inspired and nurtured by my husband, Henry Halem, and challenged by our daughter, Jessica Halem, to create work with honesty, compassion and conviction.

ON "NIGHTWALKING"

Some people who practice a process called "nightwalking" lose their fear of the dark while strengthening their peripheral vision. During these exercises, walkers said "their awareness of the world around them was broadened and they were less 'stuck' in their heads. Suddenly, fireflies seem like strobe lights. Glow worms are blinding. A quarter moon rising on a clear night could bring tears to your eyes with its brightness."*

Nightwalking, is also about trusting and training our senses as well as learning to experience and see the familiar in a new light.

* *Whole Earth Review, fall 1991*

HISTORICAL BACKGROUND

The divisive effect of the Vietnam War on American society was especially evident on campuses throughout the country. At Kent, the day after the announcement to send U.S. troops into Cambodia marked the start of a weekend of antiwar protests that began on campus and spilled into the city of Kent's downtown. Broken windows and other damage to a number of downtown businesses promoted fear, rumors, and eventually a call by the city's mayor to the governor for assistance.

The National Guard arrived Saturday night. That day some students assisted with the downtown cleanup. That night some other students set fire to the campus headquarters of the Army Reserve Officers' Training Corps (ROTC). Sunday morning the governor came to Kent and in the city's firehouse held a press conference saying the University would remain open. After a Sunday of relative calm, an antiwar rally at noon on Monday brought 2,000 to 3,000 people to the University Commons area. When the Guard gave the order to disperse, some in the crowd responded with verbal epithets and stones. The Guard answered first with tear gas, but when spring winds altered its effect, the Guard attempted to enforce the Ohio Riot Act with raised bayonets, forcing demonstrators to retreat. The Guard then changed line formation. As the Guard approached the crest of Blanket Hill, some Guardsmen turned toward the Taylor Hall parking lot, and between sixty-one and sixty-seven shots were fired. Shortly after noon, thirteen seconds of rifle fire by a contingent of twenty-eight Ohio National Guardsmen left four students, Allison Krause, Jeffrey Miller, Sandra Scheuer, and William Schroeder, dead, one permanently paralyzed and eight others wounded. Not every student was a demonstration participant or an observer. Some students were walking to and from classes. The closest wounded student was 30 yards away from the Guard, while the farthest was nearly 250 yards away. That afternoon (May 4th) University President Robert I. White ordered the University closed.

The KSU Library has dedicated a Memorial Room containing books, papers, studies and other materials relating to the events. In addition, the University has established an academic program to help students and others employ peaceful conflict resolution to resolve disputes. On May 4, 1990, the University community dedicated a permanent memorial designed by Chicago architect Bruno Ast which has the words "Inquire, Learn, Reflect" inscribed on it. Each year, an annual vigil, candlelight service, and commemoration enable the University, the Kent community, and others to privately and publicly express their feelings.

(Excerpted and reprinted with permission of Kent State University)

For more information about the May 4th archives, or to send your own personal oral history of memories surrounding May 4, 1970, please contact the Dept. of Special Collections and Archives, Kent State University, Kent, Ohio 44242. (216) 672-2270.

S

NIGHTWALKING
voices from Kent State

CAST IN ORDER OF APPEARANCE

MARGOT
CATHERINE WOODSON
FRANK WOODSON
RICHARD
SHANNON
KENT
MICHAEL WOODSON
ANONYMOUS (WOMAN)
GUARDSMAN

TIME

THE FOURTH OF MAY 1970
MAY 1995

The playwright supports the concept of non-traditional casting.

ACT ONE
At Rise

Margot stands in the spotlight.

MARGOT: It is written that God put Abraham to a test. He told him to take his beloved son, Isaac, to the land of Moriah to be offered as a sacrifice. On the third day of their journey, they left the other young men behind, and Abraham took his son ahead to the place where they would make the sacrifice. There Isaac found the wood and made the fire and then looked up at his father, whom he loved and whom he trusted and asked, "But where is the lamb, father?" Abraham looked at the boy whose eyes still burned with his youth and answered: "God will provide a lamb my son, God will provide."
(There is a clap of thunder. Frank Woodson sits at the kitchen table drinking coffee and staring at the TV which may glow or show footage. Catherine takes his plate.)
CATHERINE: Didn't you like the eggs.
FRANK: What?
(Catherine turning down the sound)
CATHERINE: You hardly touched your eggs, Frank, was there something wrong with them.
FRANK: They were fine.
CATHERINE: You hardly touched them.
FRANK: I'm waiting for the news.
CATHERINE: They said there were over 1,000 National Guard on that truck strike but they're sending them back home now.
FRANK: To school, Caty, up to that campus. Not home.

Nightwalking

CATHERINE: They said they might be leaving today. That it's probably over.
FRANK: As long as they're on that campus it's not over.
CATHERINE: Patty Miller's son, Larry, is in the guard.
FRANK: And that's supposed to make me feel better?
CATHERINE: He said those teamsters had guns out on the turnpike.
FRANK: They let that kid guard the turnpike?
CATHERINE: That kid is twenty-one.
FRANK: I got socks older than that kid.
(Catherine lets out a small laugh)
I heard that on TV.
CATHERINE: It's funny.
(Frank momentarily embraces her)
FRANK: You're the only person in the world who thinks I'm funny.
(Frank pulls away and pours coffee)
So what did Larry say was happening out there all week while he was guarding our precious turnpike.
CATHERINE: You didn't eat the toast either.
FRANK: Third shift makes me tired, not hungry,
CATHERINE: I imagine those boys are tired too. And scared.
FRANK: They better be.
CATHERINE: Patty said they were shooting right off the bridge overpass down at each other.
FRANK: When people have guns and they're pissed off – they shoot. Those truckers were real pissed off.
(Frank mimics shooting)
Pop... pop... pop.
CATHERINE: That isn't funny.
FRANK: Even truckers got their rules, Caty.
CATHERINE: Patty was very upset. The boy went in the Guard to keep away from all that fighting in Vietnam.

And now all this.
FRANK: First mistake.
CATHERINE: Nobody wants their son to go there, Frank.
FRANK: Pay or play.
CATHERINE: You just have to watch the TV to see how bad it is. To see how scared they are. What they look like when they come home.
FRANK: Nothing should have scared Larry after that father.
CATHERINE: Patty's my oldest friend.
FRANK: She still married a jerk with an arsenal.
CATHERINE: She divorced that jerk - I mean Jack - and the arsenal.
FRANK: And he was also very ugly.
CATHERINE: – and you should not speak ill of the dead.
FRANK: Jesus, I forgot the son-of-a-bitch died.
CATHERINE: Lung cancer.
(Frank pulls out a pack of cigarettes and then puts them back in his shirt)
FRANK: He was still a very ugly man.
CATHERINE: You didn't even eat your home fries. Frank, you have to eat.
FRANK: Coffee's fine.
CATHERINE: You know what the doctor said about your ulcer.
FRANK: I didn't have the cigarette, Cate, and I can't drink beer.
CATHERINE: You have to work third shift again tonight?
FRANK: Unless old Jack left me a million bucks.
CATHERINE: He didn't leave Patty or Larry a dime. Gambled it all away.
FRANK: Like I said – he was always a jerk.
(Frank paces.)
Mike here?

Nightwalking

CATHERINE: (*warmly*) It's cold in bed when you work nights.
FRANK: It's May, Caty, a very warm May and you're trying to change the subject on me. Where did Mike go?
CATHERINE: I was thinking that now that Annie's in high school I could start thinking about full-time work.
FRANK: (*abruptly*) He didn't go up there, did he?
CATHERINE: He left before I was up.
FRANK: He told me he didn't have classes today.
CATHERINE: Now you're changing the subject.
FRANK: The bills are paid, aren't they?
CATHERINE: Why don't you want to talk about me working?
FRANK: You know how I feel about it Caty. Making minimum wage you might as well stay home. That's all I have to say.
CATHERINE: Annie's going to be thinking about college soon and Mike's going to be graduating next year –
FRANK: Now, I hope to hell that's a fact.
CATHERINE: I need to do something Frank. I need to get out.
FRANK: Just a minute now, the news is coming on.
    (*Frank turns the set up*)
ANNOUNCER: "In international news, Soviet Premier Alexei Kosygin assailed President Nixon this morning for sending troops into Cambodia."
    (*CATY goes turns the TV down*)
FRANK: Leave it a minute, Caty I want to hear this.
ANNOUNCER: "Kosygin warned that the action might lead to a further complication in the international scene and a worsening of Soviet American relations."
    (*Catherine goes to turn the TV off*)
FRANK: What're you doing?
CATHERINE: It scares me.
FRANK: It's just a game.

CATHERINE: Like that Cuban missile thing, I guess that was just a little joke too because if it was supposed to scare me it worked.
FRANK: It was supposed to scare you and me and them and it did work.
CATHERINE: Too well. I still get nightmares.
FRANK: Kennedy should have sent those god damn teamsters to the Bay of Pigs and finished it off right the first time.
CATHERINE: That's not funny.
FRANK: That wasn't a joke.
CATHERINE: And that's why you are NOT the President.
FRANK: I could do it. Just let me at it. Send in the Teamsters - Mafia - hell throw in the whole fucking Ku Klux Klan and watch those guys run. What are you looking like that for?
CATHERINE: Like what?
FRANK: Like a deer caught in the headlights. Come here.
CATHERINE: I'm fine.
FRANK: You're not fine.
CATHERINE: I told you - sometimes I get scared. Today, I'm scared.
FRANK: Come here. Tell me what's making you so scared.
CATHERINE: Promise you won't laugh?
FRANK: Cross my heart.
CATHERINE: I think it could be the end of the world. And don't even think of smiling.
FRANK: The real end of the world? Like in the Bible?
CATHERINE: I don't know if it's just like they say, but I do think someday someone could get so mad they could just go in to one of those little rooms and push that button or use that phone or whatever it is that blows up everything... and it'll be all over.

Nightwalking

FRANK: Just like that? We'll all die?
CATHERINE: Yes. It could happen.
FRANK: We're all dead.
CATHERINE: You promised not to laugh.
FRANK: Look at my face. Very serious.
CATHERINE: But not scared.
FRANK: Scared but sure we're going to win this race and sure no one's ever going to push that button.
CATHERINE: How can you be so sure?
FRANK: Because we're right and they're wrong. That makes me sure.
CATHERINE: Just like that?
FRANK: It is just a test, honey, a test to keep us on our toes. Like that little Ruskie banging his shoe on the table? Just to scare us. But in the end we will win.
CATHERINE: Why?
FRANK: Cause the shoe's made here.
(Caty stares silently)
Evolution. It's 1970 not 1963 and we're a whole lot smarter. Evolution. I believe in it and you should too.
CATHERINE: I'm still scared, Frank. But I'm not helpless.
FRANK: I said I didn't have anything more to say about that.
CATHERINE: I'm not helpless. I can work. I can do something.
FRANK: We'll talk about it later.
CATHERINE: I have two good arms and two good legs. I have a brain. I'm going crazy with all the things happening everyday and I need to do something.
FRANK: We'll talk about it later. I promise, but right now I got to hear this news.
(Frank turns the set back on)
ANNOUNCER: "And now in local news. President Nixon's announcement has prompted demonstrations

throughout the country including many of our own local college campuses"...
FRANK: Now that scares me.
(Frank shuts the TV off.)
CATHERINE: I'm sure he didn't go up to the campus.
FRANK: What makes you so sure?
CATHERINE: He doesn't have any classes.
FRANK: He didn't have the last time they were up there screaming and waving but that didn't stop him from getting arrested.
CATHERINE: I'm sure he's not there.
FRANK: Then where the hell is he? Getting a haircut!
CATHERINE: He's twenty years old.
FRANK: I pay his bills. I put food on his table! I'm still his father.
CATHERINE: It's just hair.
FRANK: No, it isn't just his hair and he should have to tell me where he's going if it might get him killed.
CATHERINE: Don't talk that way, please. Don't make jokes.
FRANK: It's not a joke... believe me, this is not a joke.
(Richard walks up to an imaginary door, and knocks as Margot runs up behind him.)
MARGOT: I'm sorry I'm late.
RICHARD: It said noon in the paper.
MARGOT: I guess you're the first one here.
RICHARD: It said noon.
MARGOT: In the next century parking and traffic will run the campus. In the 90's they still just make life hell.
RICHARD: I can come back.
MARGOT: Then you'll never get a space.
(Margot unpacks her tape recorder as Richard paces nervously)
I'm actually better at this than it looks. I even worked

Nightwalking

in public television for a while - Channel 45, you might remember me, I was the one that was always asking for money.

(Margot stops a moment and poses with her microphone and starts her routine)

"We know that many of you out there have been watching Masterpiece Theatre for a lot of years before contributing... and we're just here to make you feel guilty as hell!"

RICHARD: You had different glasses.

MARGOT: They called me the "Goddess of Guilt."

RICHARD: And your hair was shorter.

MARGOT: I did that interview program no one watched.

RICHARD: You were good. I remember now. You were great. I watched.

MARGOT: I asked for money which made me feel guilty.

RICHARD: You got me to call.

MARGOT: I mean I am Jewish but I'm lousy with guilt or money.

RICHARD: Don't apologize. You got me to call.

MARGOT: My fifteen minutes of fame.

RICHARD: You look.

MARGOT: Older?

RICHARD: No... well, maybe a little.

MARGOT: I'm turning fifty next month and I should be looking older. That's one of the reasons I left television. They're more interested in what you look like than what you say. I would be out and someone would always stop me and say "Aren't you Margot Bloom from Channel 45"- and just when I was about to get in to a deep discussion about my last interview they'd throw in -"Boy you're a lot shorter than you look on TV!"

Voices from Kent State

RICHARD: I thought you were taller myself.
MARGOT: See what I mean.
RICHARD: I just watch McNeil/Lehrer now. I hate the local news.
MARGOT: I quit in '85. Too much local politics. Damn! They gave me the wrong cord.
RICHARD: I can come back.
MARGOT: Our daughter says you can never trust anyone over 30 to program your VCR.
RICHARD: Our son programs ours.
MARGOT: My husband believes it's a conspiracy by all those disgruntled AV boys.
RICHARD: Sounds like my son. He prefers computers to girls - but he's only thirteen.
MARGOT: Right now computers might seem a lot safer.
RICHARD: He makes electronic music which I hate until I remember that my parents hated my music and I hated them for not liking it.
MARGOT: Dylan?
RICHARD: I can still sing every song.
MARGOT: Today it's just talking, no singing. Give me a one... two... three for the level.
RICHARD: One... two... three for the level... You like Dylan?
MARGOT: I like Dylan, but I was partial to Baez and Judy Collins,
RICHARD: You sing?
MARGOT: Opera when I was in college. Now there's a real tool for social change. You still sing?
RICHARD: Peace Mass, that sort of thing. My son hates it.
MARGOT: I've almost got this. We took our daughter to see Peter, Paul and Mary and they sang every song I remembered.
RICHARD: Did your daughter like it?

Nightwalking

MARGOT: Hated it.

RICHARD: You look too small to sing opera.

MARGOT: Another myth. We're almost operational. The world is made up of many myths and a good number of lies.

RICHARD: I saw Madame Butterfly two years ago.

(Margot assumes Madame Butterfly stance)

MARGOT: American sailor falls in love with small Asian women, woman marries him in Japanese ceremony, sailor leaves with his ship, woman gives birth to baby, husband returns with new American wife, woman gives up baby, man leaves with new wife and new baby and Asian woman commits suicide. Like I said, a real instrument of social change.

RICHARD: You're very good.

MARGOT: I've become more dramatic in my old age. I figure it's one of the benefits.

RICHARD: What do you do now?

MARGOT: I went back to teaching.

RICHARD: You should do more TV.

MARGOT: And you should be doing the talking. Were you actually on the campus the day of the shootings?

RICHARD: No! I wasn't ... actually there.

MARGOT: Are you all right?

RICHARD: It's been twenty-five years. I didn't think it would feel like this.

MARGOT: A lot of people would like it to just go away.

RICHARD: Maybe it has been too long.

(Richard starts to pick up his briefcase.)

MARGOT: We'll be here all week.

RICHARD: (Stops) My son thinks it's all ancient history.

MARGOT: My daughter still wants to save the world so maybe there's still something left we need to say to each other.

RICHARD: Some people never move on. I worry about that. They just stay frozen. My son worries a lot more about drugs, guns and a hole in the ozone than what happened here in 1970. I don't want to grow old and angry and bitter. I want to make peace with that time, but I'm afraid that making peace means forgetting or... worse.

MARGOT: You don't seem bitter.

RICHARD: I'm a little nervous.

MARGOT: Maybe you want to do the interview by yourself. I can leave.

RICHARD: I saw the article in the paper and something snapped inside. Leave your story behind, it said. I thought, "Gee, I could do that." Like a light bulb went off in my head and it was as if it was all happening again. I'll bet it was your idea.

MARGOT: Guilty as charged.

RICHARD: It's a good idea. Leaving something behind.

MARGOT: My daughter says it's my way of holding on to things but lately I've been thinking that telling the stories might be a way of letting them go. Are you ready?

RICHARD: I never thought about where to start.

(Richard stands quietly)

MARGOT: Testing one... two... three... this is the first of our May 4th interviews... one... two... three...

(The lights dim. Michael appears casually dressed.)

MICHAEL: My father worked in a factory where they made molds for automobiles. He left high school when he was seventeen to fight in World War II and never went back. He said "D"- Day was the proudest day of

Nightwalking

his life. "Changed the world" he'd say and get that far away look I didn't understand. He didn't read books, but he read the morning newspaper like some people read the bible. When we could afford a television he used that to keep him company too. He wasn't easy with his affection though he danced with my mother in the kitchen when they were young and I even found them kissing in the hall more than once. He had a distance he had learned from his own parents who were cool, almost cruel with him. And he always said the army was a better parent than they ever were. He told me he vowed to be a better father to his son than his father had been to him and in his own way he was. He vowed his children would go to college and his dream was to see his son walking down the aisle of West Point or Annapolis and run out to shake his hand when he graduated - one man to another. Being his son was not difficult when I was young. I was on the verge of my own manhood when the silences began. We could no longer celebrate my touchdowns on a football field or making the honor roll over bowls of spaghetti and he knew it. I started to look more like him and he would often stop and watch me combing my hair which was now too long and too much like my new friends who were increasingly unlike him. That's when the silences became a scream and he knew though I was still his son, his dreams were no longer mine.

RICHARD: Stay for a while. Just until I can get started.
MARGOT: (Pause) Ready?
RICHARD: Yeah.
MARGOT: We can start with your name.
RICHARD: My name?

Voices from Kent State

MARGOT: Just say your name, first and last, right into the microphone - or you can stay anonymous. It really doesn't matter.

(Shannon stands in a spotlight holding a microphone.)

SHANNON: Hello? Hello? My name is Shannon Hofstettler. H-O-F-S-T-E-T-T-L-E-R... I'm forty -what the hell's wrong with this machine!

RICHARD: Richard... My name is Richard Perry - like the Admiral, but we're not related. Is that okay?

MARGOT: Good. Good.

SHANNON: Hello? hello? My kids always program the damn VCR because nobody but a six year old can understand it. Hello? Can anyone hear me?

MARGOT: Mr. Perry?

RICHARD: Richard is fine. *(Pause)* Do I look like an old man to you?

MARGOT: No. Why?

RICHARD: I was thirteen when my older brother left for the army and I thought he was an old man. Now I'm more than twice as old as he was when he left and I feel like that boy that watched him go.

(Margot hands him the microphone and then turns and picks up her handbag)

Aren't you going to stay?

MARGOT: You don't need me.

(Margot starts to go)

RICHARD: Do you have a story too?

MARGOT: Me? *(Pause)* I guess I do. Thanks.

(Margot walks out into the darkness)

RICHARD: On May third 1970 my father was admitted to the intensive care ward of the county hospital.

(Kent is standing holding his jacket).

Nightwalking

KENT: They told my Daddy I was too smart for my own good. They would say that and smile that smile and he knew that we'd have to leave Alabama if I was going to grow up in one piece. So one day my Daddy packed up everything and put us in his brother Arthur's car, and we came to Ohio so I could be smart and still live. Those were the choices my Daddy had in 1966. Some people don't have those choices now.

RICHARD: Actually I guess I should start at the beginning.

KENT: In 1966 my Daddy could still work at one of those good jobs in the rubber plants. The pay was good and the benefits better. He thought he had died and gone to heaven but he hadn't. They closed the plant before he was ready to grow old but was still too young to retire. Now he says to watch out. Heaven is never as close as it looks.

RICHARD: In 1970 I was twenty-one years old and I had my whole life ahead of me... if I didn't get drafted.

KENT: He fishes a lot now and keeps telling my kids to make sure they finish school.

SHANNON: I was fourteen when they shot those kids and I just have had to tell someone about it.

RICHARD: I wasn't actually on the campus that day, but I might as well have been.

SHANNON: I just had to tell someone.

RICHARD: God, I hope this is recording.

SHANNON: For years I've been thinking about it. Sometime I'll be cutting someone's cuticles or gluing on some of those really long acrylic nails and I'll have to stop what I'm doing and leave the room.

MARGOT: I wanted people to tell their stories. To have a way of leaving that day behind them. Of understanding what it all meant. Of finding the one person who would know what really happened. I wanted to know the truth.

SHANNON: I do hair and nails but I want to be a nurse someday.

RICHARD: I thought I wanted to be a musician.

SHANNON: I'm a very compassionate person.

RICHARD: But I guess in the end I was too scared to go on the road.

SHANNON: My brother was a bleeder and we still worry every day.

RICHARD: I guess some people would say I'm just a bleeding heart liberal.

SHANNON: I'm basically a pretty conservative person when it comes to things like sex... you know what I mean... people think just because you've been married and had babies that you can't still have those dreams you had when you were young - but take it from me, they don't die.

RICHARD: I lost a brother in Vietnam.

SHANNON: Somebody has to kill dreams because they can't just commit suicide.

RICHARD: I figured that was enough for one family to give.

SHANNON: Then two years ago my husband Jason left me after we lost our trailer in that last big tornado, so I know all about dreams.

RICHARD: I was student teaching junior high school science.

MARGOT: I was a newlywed in 1969.

SHANNON: That tornado was sort of the last straw for Jason who lost his job when the plant moved south.

RICHARD: I know all the jokes about junior high kids and most of them are as right as they are wrong. But besides keeping me out of the war, it kept me in touch with myself - with my dreams.

Nightwalking

SHANNON: We lost everything in that wind. Everything.

MARGOT: My parents lost their business in 1968. Everything.

SHANNON: But I have my children.

MARGOT: The war was everywhere that year. My old boyfriends were going off to Canada if they couldn't get into graduate school - or shooting their toes off. I wasn't sure I ever wanted children. Then I met my husband and everything changed.

SHANNON: Sometimes I think having those twins is all I have.

RICHARD: My mother was against that war all the way. My father wasn't. He believed in it to his last breath even though we didn't talk about it anymore. At least not in the house. We couldn't. Not after my brother died and they sent what was left of him home in a box. At least we think it was him. They told us we would have to trust them. That we could never open it. Just trust that it was really him in there. And we did. What else could we do. We needed him home.

MARGOT: Somewhere along the way I made a good life, wanted a child and changed my life all over again.

RICHARD: They were looking for men teachers, role models they said, and they needed science teachers – all that racing to the moon you know. I also ran track, even won a few state championships so I had this coaching thing to fall back on. Believe me, in those days every little bit helped.

SHANNON: Jason didn't have a lot to fall back on. Who am I kidding. Jason didn't have anything to fall back on or look forward to but I didn't see it. Hell, I didn't see anything but love.

RICHARD: There's just no way to describe the mind of a 12 or thirteen year old. They're so raw - they either come out of those years stronger - or they don't come out at all.

MARGOT: My husband was a photographer. Coming to Ohio was his first teaching job. When they called he thought it was Penn State. We'd never been west of the Pennsylvania line.

RICHARD: Sometimes those are the best years of their lives.

MARGOT: 1969 was the best year of our lives.

RICHARD: Sometimes they're the worst.

MARGOT: Then suddenly it was the worst.

RICHARD: They're always in love.

MARGOT: We were really in love.

RICHARD: And then there's always the sex.

MARGOT: And we were really in lust.

RICHARD: Love and hate are the strongest emotions in their lives.

MARGOT: That first year was like a roller coaster. Moving, marrying – yeah, we did it in that order. I mean it was the sixties.

RICHARD: And sometimes there's no difference.

MARGOT: We figured we were coming to a new place and we should start off married.

RICHARD: The world can be a terrible place when you're just starting out.

MARGOT: It was a wonderful time to be in love when your husband's too old for the draft.

RICHARD: My brother went to Vietnam in '67. He said it was a special kind of hell and I believed him. He was my big brother and though he was grown up and gone before I had a chance to really know him, I knew he'd never lie to me.

SHANNON: I said, Hell Jason, you knew they were closing those factories since we were back in junior high. You

Nightwalking

should have prepared. "Prepared," he says, looking at me like I was from Mars. "Who prepares for hell."

RICHARD: A lot of my students ran to the army - begged into the navy - dreamed of flying for the air force and dropped out early to get there faster. The only time they were sad was when they couldn't get anybody to take them in. Then they would show up back at the school wondering what the hell they were going to do with their lives.

SHANNON: "Who prepares for hell," and I'm supposed to answer that?

RICHARD: They say the miners took canaries down with them into the mines to warn them when there was gas. Just watch the canaries, they said. And when they die - run like hell.

SHANNON: Jason had beautiful eyes when we met – full of hope.

RICHARD: Sometimes when I look into the eyes of those kids they look just like those canaries.

SHANNON: Believe me, I would never have fallen in love with a boy with no hope.

RICHARD: So much hope in September and by June it's gone.

SHANNON: We may have only been thirteen when we met - but he had hope. And dreams like the kind you see in the movies.

RICHARD: They do want to be somebody.

SHANNON: We both did.

RICHARD: They need to be somebody.

SHANNON: We needed each other.

RICHARD: When I get them they're only thirteen.

SHANNON: When you're thirteen you think you know everything. Especially about sex. And if you don't know it, you fake it, which is mostly everything since you really don't know nothing and when you're thirteen sex is everything you think about - at least if you have nothing else to live for. Hell, we thought we knew a lot more about sex than anything else and we didn't know anything about anything else at all.

RICHARD: But by June it's gone. Dead as fish eyes.

SHANNON: He wanted to be something then. We both did. We were thirteen. What the hell did we know.

MARGOT: Before we came here we'd never been west of Pennsylvania.

RICHARD: Just old enough to think about the world and where they want to be in it.

SHANNON: We thought Ohio was the center of the Universe.

MARGOT: I thought Ohio was just one big hay field.

RICHARD: But not old enough to be defeated by it. No, not yet.

SHANNON: Then Jason hit high school and he found out he wasn't so good at much out there and I just made hair my life.

KENT: I was a Junior in college that May and I was on scholarship. Most white folks asked what position I played and though I kept saying academic, they kept hearing athletic, so I gave up and told my Daddy everything was fine. I told myself I didn't have to take this shit, but I took it anyway.

SHANNON: Coming up here to this place saved my life. Jason said it made him nervous, like everyone thought he was trash, but I told him nobody could tell who was trash 'til you graduated. My older girlfriend had a car and we came up all the time. We'd say we were at work or baby - sitting but we weren't. We were just hoping some of that smart would rub off on us.

(The ANONYMOUS WOMAN starts

21

Nightwalking

across the stage clutching her handbag.)

ANONYMOUS: I came to talk about what happened when they shot those children because it wasn't all they said.

KENT: The night the Governor called out the National Guard a bunch of the brothers got together to talk.

ANONYMOUS: I knew some of them that were there and some were innocent and some weren't. Some were lost before and some after. I came to tell you about the one I knew – but you can't use my name.

KENT: Everybody says they remember where they were when they heard Kennedy was shot, well I remember where I was when I heard those little black girls were killed in that church in Alabama. I remember because I was in that church a hundred times before and I could have been there that day, too. I remember what it looked like, how the wood smelled and what the pews felt like under your fingers. I remember because it could have been me. My mother and father are God fearing people so I don't ask them why those children died.

ANONYMOUS: I lived through a lot of dying in my time but I never expected shooting here.

KENT: After they sent in the soldiers, some of the brothers talked about whether we should stay on the campus. Time and death had made us a lot less trusting than those little girls.

ANONYMOUS: No, not here where I worked.

KENT: There were the two Kennedy brothers and Medger, Martin and Malcolm and a lot of other people with names I have forgotten. I remember dying in lots of colors.

ANONYMOUS: I've lost my husband to the diabetes, one child to high blood pressure and a grandchild in an

Voices from Kent State

automobile so I know about dying. I didn't know about it that day, but I was told there would be trouble and so I wasn't there.

KENT: I always thought it was safe at school till they brought in those troops, and then I didn't sleep all night.

ANONYMOUS: I watch the TV news every night and I worry everyday. There's a lot of violence out there. A lot of guns.

KENT: I had memories of nice scrubbed white boys with guns.

ANONYMOUS: A lot of dying everyday.

KENT: No dogs or hoods or firehoses to threaten but any self-respecting black man knows the Klan didn't need a gun to kill you and the government did.

ANONYMOUS: No, I was told there would be trouble and I believed it.

MICHAEL: On May 4th 1970 I was three days shy of my twenty-first birthday. I had won an appointment to West Point when I was eighteen and left when I was nineteen - that was the first time my Dad had stopped talking to me. The silence lasted almost two months. After I moved back home, I got a part-time job, started attending the University but I still didn't know what I wanted to do with my life. My father was impatient for me to find myself in him and make him happy and less lonely. But I was falling in love with questions he could not or would not answer and every new question was like a bone in his throat and every new answer hung around our house like that war outside that was now our war too. Everyday there were new wounds and like that other war, there seemed no honorable way out.

(The lights will go up and Michael will

> *become transformed and move effortlessly into the past. There is the sound of a car stopping and a door opening and closing)*

CATHERINE: See, Frank, here's Michael now.

MICHAEL: Even now, so many years later, when I speak about those times I can feel his voice rising in my head, my stomach drawing tightly into knots as she holds out her hand to me, my whole body recoiling as we are drawn desperately together even as we were driven inevitably apart.

CATHERINE: *(Running towards Michael holding out her hand)* You're home, I told your father –

MICHAEL: I can't stay.

CATHERINE: Where are you going now?

MICHAEL: I'll call you later.

> *(Michael starts to leave but Frank stops him.)*

FRANK: Your mother asked you where you were going.

MICHAEL: Out.

FRANK: She deserves an answer.

MICHAEL: What difference does it make where I am going?

FRANK: It makes a difference if you're going up there.

MICHAEL: Either way I am going to get it from you, aren't I?

CATHERINE: You promised you wouldn't go up there again if there was going to be trouble.

MICHAEL: That's my school, Mom. It's where I live.

FRANK: You live here, son, unless you've moved out.

CATHERINE: Please, Michael, your father and I don't want trouble.

MICHAEL: I told you I wouldn't get in to trouble.

FRANK: You just said you don't have classes. Why would you go there if you don't want trouble and you don't have classes.

MICHAEL: You don't learn everything in a classroom.
FRANK: Is that what they're teaching you now? How to stay out of class? Or is that what your friends are teaching you.
CATHERINE: I don't think that's what he means Frank.
FRANK: Maybe you don't need a real education anymore. Maybe you've already learned everything you need to know.
CATHERINE: We're just concerned, that's all.
MICHAEL: I don't want to be hurt and I don't want to hurt anyone. But there's more to life than what you read in a book and there's more to living than watching it all on TV.
CATHERINE: There are terrible things happening out there. I'm afraid.
MICHAEL: Maybe I'm afraid too.
FRANK: I didn't think you were afraid of anything.
CATHERINE: Let him speak Frank, please. What are you afraid of?
MICHAEL: Of doing nothing. Of watching this country fall apart. Of seeing us become our own worst nightmare.
FRANK: And what do you think you're doing about that running around in the streets waving your arms in the air holding up signs and doing God knows what else?
MICHAEL: I'm trying to do my part, that's all.
FRANK: You think you can change the whole damn government by yourself. You think you can stop that war when nobody else up there can? You think you're God!
CATHERINE: Stop it Frank. He didn't say that! He just said he wanted to try.
MICHAEL: I need to do something so I can live with myself.
FRANK: And what are me and your mother supposed to live

Nightwalking

with?
MICHAEL: I'm doing this for all of us, not just me. All of us.
   (Michael picks up his bag)
   I gotta go.
FRANK: I don't want you to go there today Michael.
MICHAEL: Just like that?
CATHERINE: We're just really worried.
FRANK: If you don't have any business there you don't go.
MICHAEL: I have business.
FRANK: I mean your education.
MICHAEL: So do I.
   (Michael packs his knapsack)
CATHERINE: Michael, please, promise me you'll leave if it looks like trouble.
FRANK: If you go there and you don't have classes, you don't have to come back here.
MICHAEL: Is that an ultimatum?
FRANK: If you want it to be.
CATHERINE: He's our son.
MICHAEL: Fine.
   (Michael starts out and Catherine stops him)
CATHERINE: No, you can't leave this way. I know your father's upset and I'm upset too. But I won't have our son thinking he can't come home again. I can't live like that. I hate what's going on up there and I don't know anymore what's wrong about the government, but I know what's right in my home and I can't turn my son away from me. Do you hear me, Michael? I can't stop you from going up to that campus today, even though I want to tell you not to go. But I can't do it. Even though I want to keep you here with me – forever if it means you'll be safe, but I know I can't do that either. So you go up there if you have to, but you

come back home when it's over. No matter what happens, you come back here.
(Frank walks away)
MICHAEL: I promise I'll leave if there's trouble.
(Michael kisses his mother, walks around his father and exits)
MARGOT: That morning I kissed my husband as usual and went to teach school.
GUARDSMAN: I was in the National Guard in 1970 and my parents were happy I could stay in school, earn some money for my tuition and not get my head blown off in Vietnam.
MARGOT: We didn't talk about the soldiers that morning.
GUARDSMAN: We didn't talk about the war, but it was always there.
MARGOT: But they were there and we knew it.
KENT: Some of the brothers said to leave this protest to those boys on the hill with their guns and those kids standing up to them with rocks in one hand and their fingers raised up like a weapon on the other. I said it, too, but I don't know if I believed it.
GUARDSMAN: We knew lots of people whose kids were there - even my cousin Barbara was going over as nurse.
KENT: More brothers going over to Nam everyday. Nobody came back like they went.
GUARDSMAN: We lived outside of Pittsburgh and my Dad seemed a lot more worried about the jobs leaving than the boys coming home. He was a good man, but he understood work not war.
RICHARD: It's important to listen to be a good teacher.
KENT: Nobody was listening to anybody anymore.
GUARDSMAN: The Valley was humming like the old days. But it wasn't the old days and nothing was ever going

Nightwalking

to be exactly the way it was before.

RICHARD: You got to make them feel a part of the process.

GUARDSMAN: I'd been on duty with the Teamsters before Kent and I was tired. They told us the old ROTC building on campus was burning and the protesters were throwing rocks at the fireman and police, and cutting the hoses. I hadn't slept in my bed for a week but when they told us to move out, I went. It wasn't Vietnam, so why was I so scared?

RICHARD: Or you might lose them.

GUARDSMAN: The old ROTC building wasn't much of a building, but it was a helluva symbol.

KENT: I'd seen them out there Saturday night, the fireman trying to keep the water going, the flames leaping up and licking the sky – and those dark figures cutting the hoses.

ANONYMOUS: I remember that building since I came here.

KENT: That building was history.

GUARDSMAN: That Sunday morning was bright and sunny and the smell of the burned building still hung in the air. I saw a lot of faces I knew. Faculty and students, boyfriends and girlfriends, dogs and frisbees. It looked a lot more like a picnic than a protest. Until the Governor showed up at the firehouse.

ANONYMOUS: I'm a Democrat myself so I hadn't voted for the man.

MARGOT: The Governor said those protesters couldn't continue to set fire to buildings worth 5 and 10 million dollars.

ANONYMOUS: They said that old building was worth about $35,000 - twice as much as my home. I was really surprised since my home looked a whole lot better.

RICHARD: The Governor said these people move from one

campus to another and terrorize a community.
SHANNON: He called them worse than those brownshirts...
ANONYMOUS: And the Communists...
KENT: And the nightriders.
GUARDSMAN: They're the worst type of people we harbor in America, he said.
MARGOT: And we're going to eradicate the problem.
ANONYMOUS: I was afraid. I'm not ashamed to say that now.
SHANNON: I didn't know what the hell ERADICATE was supposed to mean or I probably would have been a whole lot more scared than I was.
MARGOT: The Governor came down that morning and he changed the mission of the Guard from protecting property and lives to breaking up any assembly, peaceful or otherwise.
KENT: That's when I started thinking about leaving.
MARGOT: Pounding his fist repeatedly he said,
RICHARD: "We're going to employ every force of law that we have under our authority... We are going to employ every weapon possible."
KENT: Any self respecting nigger in 1970 knew that white boys in uniforms don't carry weapons for our health.
GUARDSMAN: I was a student at Kent but I lived in a private home off-campus and the people liked me because I was clean cut, clean shaven and in the military.
ANONYMOUS: You'd be surprised how many people in the town used to talk about how nice it would be to have a university with no students.
RICHARD: When that building went up in flames and they broke those windows something snapped.
KENT: I was a nigger and a student which made me a nigger twice.
GUARDSMAN: When we arrived on campus that Saturday

Nightwalking

night we knew there were guns out in the town and we were told to keep those students up on that campus so nobody got shot.

RICHARD: Nobody was listening to anybody.

GUARDSMAN: I had a friend who was in my unit. He got in trouble and they sent him over to Nam the next weekend. He didn't follow the rules and they sent him over because that's what happened when you messed up.

KENT: Why didn't somebody guess those guns were loaded.

GUARDSMAN: No questions, no excuses. Just "Here's your ticket to Saigon." We knew the rules. We were already a well trained unit – maybe some others weren't – but the message was simple – carry a gun at Kent State or in Da Nang.

RICHARD: It's important to listen to be a good teacher.

GUARDSMAN: I just had to make it through one more hour.

RICHARD: It's important to listen when people are talking to you so you don't miss what they have to say.

GUARDSMAN: I was happy because I didn't want to be carrying a gun on that hill one minute longer than I had to.

(Catherine and Frank stand alone in the kitchen)

CATHERINE: You've always said he was a good boy.

GUARDSMAN: I was a hunter since I was ten. I knew how to hold a gun and track a deer. I wasn't afraid of guns. I respected them.

CATHERINE: Frank, are you listening to me?

GUARDSMAN: But this was no forest. And there were no deer.

CATHERINE: You always said Michael was a good son.

FRANK: Because then he was a good son.

CATHERINE: Don't turn away, Frank. Everything's going to be all right.

FRANK: How can you be so sure?

CATHERINE: He promised.

ANNOUNCER: "President Nixon said today that the United States is not widening the war"

FRANK: Everybody lies Caty! That's the only thing you can ever be sure of.

(Margot stands in spotlight).

MARGOT: I got up that Monday morning and took my shower, dressed, ate my breakfast and kissed my husband good-bye as if it was just another Monday. I knew he was going to the campus and I knew there were soldiers there. I had seen them, walked among them, but as I drove out of town, I wasn't afraid. No, I wasn't afraid at all.

BLACKOUT

END OF ACT ONE

Nightwalking

ACT TWO
At Rise

Frank stands in the dark kitchen. Richard walks onstage.

RICHARD: The cross country coach dropped dead of a heart attack. Boom! Dead on the first day of my student teaching. Left a wife and two small children. Had a physical six months before but it didn't matter. The doctor said he was a walking time bomb. Everybody said it was a tragedy – but not a disaster. A disaster would have been if the football coach had died.

KENT: I was at the university on an academic scholarship because my father wouldn't have it any other way.

RICHARD: I ran track in high school but nobody gave a damn.

KENT: My Dad said those bigots might cheer you on the field but that doesn't mean they want you to live next door to them.

RICHARD: The only thing anyone gives a damn about is football.

KENT: No, he'd smile, curling that upper lip, they don't mind us running that pigskin or fighting their wars. Hell, he'd laugh, they might even like us fighting their wars.

RICHARD: My brother was a big star. All-American everything.

KENT: Kill two Niggers with one bullet if you're lucky, he said 'cause the enemy – the enemy is always the nigger.

RICHARD: Everyone loved him except the Viet Cong.

KENT: So you do it on your brains, he told me, and then if you're smart enough – maybe you won't have to fight for them, run for them, or live with them.

SHANNON: I loved this place. It's hard to explain now, but I really felt free here.
ANONYMOUS: I worked up here on the campus until I retired.
SHANNON: We'd cut out of school to sit in the cafeteria and hang out.
ANONYMOUS: I worked preparing food for the cafeteria.
SHANNON: Drinking pop, eating junk food and french fries.
ANONYMOUS: It was a good job. A decent job.
SHANNON: When I was here I thought I'd died and gone to heaven.
ANONYMOUS: Vegetables and chicken, meat loaf with gravy and mashed potatoes. Good food. It's important for young people.
SHANNON: Eating from those machines.
ANONYMOUS: I hated to see those children eating from machines.
SHANNON: I had my first cigarette here but I don't smoke anymore. My girl's got asthma - but not from me.
ANONYMOUS: And those girls smoking cigarettes would break my heart.
SHANNON: They said it was probably from the mold. Ohio has a lot of mold including some wild mushrooms growing right in the basement of my parents' house. That's where we lived til we got our trailer which didn't have a basement. Not having a basement is hell in Ohio. When the tornado comes there's no place to hide.
ANONYMOUS: I like my food fresh and I cooked for those students just like they were my own family. That's the only way I work.
SHANNON: There were plenty of mushrooms in that house. Not that I would ever think of eating them. My friend

Nightwalking

Brinna said if you eat the wrong kind of mushrooms you can become a vegetable... and that's no joke. No, I want all my food frozen or wrapped in plastic.

ANONYMOUS: God didn't mean for human beings to eat their food frozen or wrapped in plastic.

SHANNON: I was smoking those cigarettes for women. The ones that made you look so cool and they had the little gifts when you bought a whole carton. I swear I wouldn't have started if they hadn't looked so good. And I didn't think they were allowed to sell you something that could really kill you.

ANONYMOUS: You have to cook with love 'cause bad cooking can kill you.

SHANNON: I left home when I was sixteen. Things just kept getting worse so I just packed up and left.

ANONYMOUS: I was sixteen in Charlotte, North Carolina when I took my first job cooking. Moved up here when I was nineteen to live with my Aunt. I met my husband when he started working on the automobile assembly line and we married when I was twenty. We had three children, two girls and a boy.

SHANNON: Jason and me got married when I was nineteen.

ANONYMOUS: We moved here when my children were ready for school and I started working in the elementary school cafeteria.

SHANNON: You wouldn't believe the little town I grew up in.

ANONYMOUS: My husband thought a small town was a better place to raise a family.

SHANNON: It was so small they had to bus us to another school with kids from two other towns smaller than mine.

ANONYMOUS: Sometimes he was right.

SHANNON: It was hard to make friends and sometimes those

kids were meaner than my own family.

ANONYMOUS: My husband was a very good man. I miss him everyday.

SHANNON: My Dad drank a lot and I don't miss him at all.

ANONYMOUS: I worked at the elementary first.

SHANNON: My Mom just took it all. The drinking and the fighting.

ANONYMOUS: But I didn't have seniority and I was the first to go.

SHANNON: I'm telling you, she didn't ask for it.

ANONYMOUS: I went up to the college where they had civil service.

SHANNON: The truth is that she did have a tongue that could rip your heart out, but I never read where that was a capital offense.

ANONYMOUS: The civil service made me feel safe.

SHANNON: Believe me, she knew just where to go and I can show you scars that'll never go away. But I can't think that's enough to knock her teeth out or turn her eyes black or break her nose. Hell, no, I don't believe it's in the constitution that you have the right to knock someone's brains around just because they're a bitch.

ANONYMOUS: And when I got old enough I retired.

SHANNON: I never took abuse from nobody, ever, and yes, I always looked like this.

ANONYMOUS: My oldest is gone now - and my husband too. I just need enough to take care of myself and leave a little behind for my grandchildren.

SHANNON: My mother's dead now too. Killed defending six gas pumps and a cash box with fifty-five dollars in it. Nobody's life should come down to fifty-five dollars. In the end - we even buried her in that damn Quickie Mart uniform.

Nightwalking

ANONYMOUS: My husband drank a little wine on the holidays and lived long enough to collect two months pension.

SHANNON: The truth is that I never did find out why she stayed with him so long. Now I can never ask.

ANONYMOUS: The truth is that people should have a little more in this life. But that isn't always what life is about.

RICHARD: The truth is that if you can get the students young enough they still have hope. And if you don't lie to them they can keep it.

KENT: The truth is that nobody seems to know how things really happened anywhere you really care about.

(Michael runs in breathless and goes for the TV)

MICHAEL: Did you hear what happened?

FRANK: Leave it off.

CATHERINE: You're okay now, that's all that matters, right Frank?

MICHAEL: Don't you care?

FRANK: No!

CATHERINE: Everything's all right now.

MICHAEL: They shot four students, Mom. Nothing's all right.

CATHERINE: We heard it was soldiers, Michael.

FRANK: They shot the Guard is what happened.

MICHAEL: No, it's not!

CATHERINE: That's what we heard son.

MICHAEL: You heard it wrong, damn it! It's a lie. They didn't shoot any Guard. They shot students. The fuckers shot them dead.

FRANK: Watch your mouth son. You're not out on the street now.

Voices from Kent State

MICHAEL: I saw it... damn it... I was there. It was terrible. Terrible.

MARGOT: They came in to my class and told me they had shot four national Guardsman dead on the campus.

KENT: People lie when they don't know the truth and they lie when they do. It just depends on whether they want the truth or need the lie.

MARGOT: They said the university had been closed, there was martial law in the town and I couldn't go home.

KENT: Sometimes it's lying for the good, sometimes it's just lies. It doesn't matter unless it hurts you and it doesn't make any difference unless it helps you -

MARGOT: I didn't know what to believe at first.

KENT: Lies come in all colors.

ANONYMOUS: It was right in the paper that it was soldiers shot and they were looking in the river for the gun that started it all.

KENT: A gun they never found and shots no one heard.

ANONYMOUS: It was right on the front page that afternoon.

MARGOT: The phone lines were jammed.

ANONYMOUS: If you don't believe the newspaper, who can you believe.

MARGOT: I kept trying to get my husband but all I got was a busy signal. And now I'm scared. Real scared.

ANONYMOUS: This young girl I want to tell you about worked with me in the cafeteria was probably up there on that hill. If there was a gun she probably knew who fired it. But they never found the gun and I never saw that girl again.

MICHAEL: No, you heard it wrong, it was students who were killed. And they were just going to class.

FRANK: Now that just shows you it's a lie because if they were just going to class, God damn it, they wouldn't be

Nightwalking

dead.
(Michael moves to the TV)
Leave that damn thing off!

MARGOT: The roads coming into town were empty and quiet except for the sound of the helicopters overhead. *(Pause)* I thought it was the end of the world.

RICHARD: My mother called me at my school and told me to come to the hospital. It was almost noon and my father had been in the intensive care ward with a stroke. The doctors told her he was now in God's hands.

MICHAEL: Dead soldiers is what you expect, isn't it.

FRANK: I don't like dead soldiers any better than I like dead students!

MICHAEL: But it's what you expected.

FRANK: And what did you expect when you went up there? A welcoming committee?

MICHAEL: You think they got what they deserved, don't you.

FRANK: You said that, not me.

MICHAEL: But that's what you think, isn't it?

FRANK: Now you know what I think too. If you're so damn smart how come you didn't know what was going to happen up there.
(Michael seems frozen. Frank continues.)
Well?

MICHAEL: Pay or play, shut up and listen, don't talk back, do what you're told, do your duty, follow the leader, and if they don't listen just blow their heads off, one, two, three, four, and then we can all go home and go back to our lives like nothing ever happened.

FRANK: Are you done?

MICHAEL: If you all love this god damn war so much then why don't you just go over and fight it and leave the

rest of us alone -
FRANK: (*Interrupting*) -you think it's all a game - fucking hair down to your butts waving your little fingers in the air, well it's not a game, god damn it, and I won't have you and your friends -
> (*Frank grabs a kitchen knife and grabs Michael by his long hair. Catherine watches in horror as Frank holds Michael down at his knees, the knife above his head*)

CATHERINE: Oh, God, Frank please don't hurt him.
> (*They all freeze*)

MARGOT: So Abraham and Isaac went together to the place that God had told him.
RICHARD: And together the father and the son built the altar.
ANONYMOUS: And they laid the wood down...
GUARDSMAN: Then Abraham bound Isaac,
KENT: And laid his son upon that wood.
SHANNON: And the father stretched forth his hand,
KENT: Then lifted his knife to slay his son,
SHANNON: Whom he loved,
TOGETHER: And for whom he was willing to sacrifice everything.
MICHAEL: What are you waiting for? If that's what you want to do, damn it, just go ahead and do it. DO IT!
MARGOT: But the angel of God called Abraham to lay down the knife - and he did.
> (*Frank lowers the knife and Michael falls to the floor as Catherine rushes to him*)

CATHERINE: Thank God, it's over.
> (*Frank starts to walk out and Michael stops him*)

MARGOT: And God commanded Abraham to sacrifice the lamb instead.

Nightwalking

MICHAEL: Dad? Is it really over?

MARGOT: I was teaching school that day when they ran into my class and told me I couldn't go home.

CATHERINE: Look at him. He's our son.

ANONYMOUS: This young girl I worked with was a good girl. Then she met this boy and everything was different.

MARGOT: After some anti-war demonstrators had been arrested, one columnist wrote in the local paper that - Quote, some of the demonstrators who called themselves non-conformists were the usual disheveled lot with torn clothes which hadn't seen a cleaner or wash for months: sandals, combat boots or moccasins; and, of course, dirty uncombed long hair. Unquote.

ANONYMOUS: The boy said this revolution would be the real one.

MARGOT: On the other hand, the reporter noted, a few of the females seemed well-bred, properly dressed young women, but the majority were as unattractive as the men.

ANONYMOUS: This time they would get it right.

KENT: It was warm that Sunday the guard came on campus.

ANONYMOUS: I know there are things wrong with this country. I know. But that boy scared me. He still does.

KENT: The soldiers tried hard not to look at the young girls. The kids tried hard not to see those guns.

MARGOT: True, the reporter wrote - clothes don't make the man, but these clothes were something else!

ANONYMOUS: I've heard plenty of crazy Republicans and Democrats but he didn't sound like any of them.

KENT: They just kept flashing their peace signs at those guns. They didn't get it at all.

ANONYMOUS: After a while the girl stopped talking to me

Voices from Kent State

about the war, but she was still taking care of that boy while she getting to be all skin and bones. She was full of secrets now too. Then that building burned and she came to see me in the cafeteria. It was Sunday and I only served one meal. She looked so frightened that when she made me promise to go home and not come back til the soldiers were gone, I said yes.

KENT: The black students had already walked off this campus once. But it wasn't about the fight in Vietnam. No, it was about the fight to make us part of a system that acted like we didn't exist. We walked and we got something. Not everything. But enough.

ANONYMOUS: She kissed me right on my cheek and disappeared.

KENT: I never saw any faces like mine in books except Harriet Tubman and Booker T. Maybe it was too late for us, but we walked for the ones that were still to come.

ANONYMOUS: I don't want to leave my name but you can be sure I'm telling you the truth.

KENT: So when America marched into Cambodia I knew it wasn't because we loved Asians. And when they sent those guards up to the campus it wasn't because they loved students.

ANONYMOUS: She knew something was going to happen. She told me to go. I think lots of people knew something bad could happen. Why even the President of the University was gone.

KENT: Those guns were loaded. They are always loaded.

ANONYMOUS: Then the girl - Mary was her name - was gone.

RICHARD: Even though some things between us would never be settled, he was my father and he was dying and I

Nightwalking

had to go.

ANONYMOUS: I don't have to leave my name do I?

KENT: Bang. Bang. Bang. Bang.

RICHARD: My Dad didn't think much of teaching as a profession.

ANONYMOUS: It's like a family up here too.

RICHARD: He used to say that those who can, do - those who can't, teach. A lot of people still say that. They think teaching is a joke, and they pay them that way.

ANONYMOUS: And no one likes you to talk bad things about the family.

KENT: One... two... three... four.

MARGOT: My father loved Richard Nixon. I loved my father but I didn't understand him anymore. I loved him, but I hated Richard Nixon.

ANONYMOUS: Keep the bad things inside the family is what they feel.

RICHARD: But there was a magic inside my head when I was in the classroom.

ANONYMOUS: I really just have that one story.

RICHARD: And that magic slowly was just one more gulf between us.

ANONYMOUS: But maybe it needs to be told.

MARGOT: I left for college in 1962 just as the family business was already going to pieces - but nobody said a word.

FRANK: If you had just stayed in that damned Academy...

MARGOT: My mother just started to water down my father's scotch and I learned to be afraid of being home.

FRANK: You wouldn't be worried about who was going to shoot you - but who you were going to shoot!

MICHAEL: Look at me Dad. For once really look at me.

MARGOT: Dad sold his business to a man who made helicopters for the Vietnam war. He made a fortune and my father went broke. The man took the business - as a tax loss, and it was legal. An amazing country when losing money was better than making something. It didn't make sense then and it doesn't make sense now. So my parents' retirement was no retirement at all. My father sat in a chair in Florida from September until December of 1969 thinking he was safe. But by the spring of 1970, the business was gone, kaput, closed its doors and he was left staring at a quarter of a million dollars of worthless paper.

ANONYMOUS: I came to tell what I know but you can't use my name.

MARGOT: He never really worked again. But he didn't blow his brains out either.

RICHARD: Funny how something that could make you feel so good - could separate you from the people you loved the most.

MARGOT: He just sat in front of his television with a glass of scotch in one hand and his life in the other and watched Richard Nixon til he died.

MICHAEL: Just who was I going to kill?

MARGOT: I wonder what I would have done if my life had disappeared.

MICHAEL: He looked at me and he knew...

CATHERINE: You're home now. That's all that matters. Tell him you're happy that he's all right. Frank! Tell him.

MICHAEL: We were strangers.

CATHERINE: Maybe we can't all agree about this war but we can still be a family.

MICHAEL: You have to believe things can change.

FRANK: I don't like change.

CATHERINE: Your father and I are just trying to make a good life for you and your sister.

Nightwalking

FRANK: I don't like the hair. I can't get used to the talk and sex and the drugs. I don't like the world I fought for and I don't know what to do about it.

MICHAEL: You used to be interested in talking to me.

FRANK: You used to be interesting to talk to. We had things to do together. You had good hands. We don't play the same games anymore.

MICHAEL: You don't want to talk to me anymore.

FRANK: You changed. I didn't.

(Frank walks into the darkness.)

RICHARD: It was very quiet in my house. My Mother hated the war, my father supported it. At some point the arguments stopped and so did the talking.

MICHAEL: Suddenly my father and mother were alone in the room and I was gone from the discussion.

FRANK: I believe that if this protesting keeps going on there will be more bodies laying in the streets of America than there will ever be laying in the streets of Hanoi.

CATHERINE: How can you say that?

FRANK: You can't disagree every time you don't like something. Sometimes you just have to shut up and take what you're given.

CATHERINE: But you don't think we should hurt them, Frank. That isn't what you mean, is it?

FRANK: Don't push me on this Catherine.

CATHERINE: But I want to understand. Frank I need to understand.

FRANK: Don't push me Caty

CATHERINE: I just want you to tell me how you feel about those students and the soldiers -

FRANK: (interrupting) - if they have to shoot a few to shut them up then do it! Is that what you want to hear because that's how I feel. If it takes some dead ones to make the peace then that's what I mean.

CATHERINE: But you always said that even though you and your father disagreed, in the end you still loved each other.

FRANK: (*Pause*) I lied.

MICHAEL: I saw her back stiffen and her shoulders fall. His eyes went dark. There are things we only learn about those we love at the end of it. I knew she would never leave him, I also knew she would never love him quite the same way again.

ANONYMOUS: They never found a gun and they said it wasn't the students who shot but they don't know everything and they don't say everything they know. You can be sure of that. I mean really know why it happened. But I think that Mary knew. I do.

KENT: When you're a black man you learn early to respect the gun. You don't go up against it unless you're willing to use it - or run from it. That weekend - a lot of the brothers left.

ANONYMOUS: Her name was Mary Eugenia, but everyone called her Mary and even though she said she didn't know God anymore - she told me to stay home from work and I did.

KENT: We have two children and no guns in our house. I expect my children to go to college. I want to believe that their lives will be better. I need to believe that things will get better.

RICHARD: On the day of the shooting, I would have been on campus but my class was giving me a party - or I might have been lying in a bed next to my father in that hospital ward.

KENT: In the end I didn't leave. It was my school, too - my country and my war.

Nightwalking

ANONYMOUS: Mary's father had been rich and they had lived in a big house. Then something terrible happened and he died by his own hand and she lost her mother from the breast cancer the year after. I love God, but God is a mystery.

MICHAEL: Twenty-five years later my father is dying of bone cancer. He is old and frail and his lungs have forgotten how to do their work. His mind fades in and out, and sometimes, when they give him the drugs, he speaks of times long gone.

ANONYMOUS: I remember watching the news that night and wondering where she was and what she was doing.

KENT: Bang... Bang... Bang... Bang.

(shooting in slow motion)

ANONYMOUS: I know she stopped caring about most things by the time that boy got to her.

MICHAEL: Of "D"-day and his wedding.

KENT: Bang... Bang... Bang...

ANONYMOUS: But she never stopped caring about me.

MICHAEL: Of work and my childhood.

KENT: Bang... bang... bang...

MICHAEL: And the day those students died.

ANONYMOUS: I don't know why those children were shot, but I believe that God does and Mary might too.

MARGOT: I have a recurring dream that Abraham has taken Isaac up that mountain. I see him with his hands raised high above Isaac's head, the knife shining, the boy's eyes full of terror... and I try to remember what is supposed to happen next because I have heard this story every year of my life, and I know that something is supposed to happen to save him, but in my dream, nothing is happening and I am afraid.

RICHARD: I was on my way to the hospital to see my father.

He had a stroke and my mother called me at the school and told me to come right away. He was failing - that's how she put it.

MARGOT: I run to find God or the Angel or my Mother because I am afraid that nothing will happen. And then I wake up.

ANONYMOUS: I worked with that girl two years and I saw her change.

SHANNON: Jason changed everyday we were married. He wasn't -

ANONYMOUS: She wasn't -

SHANNON: The boy -

ANONYMOUS: The girl -

SHANNON: I loved.

MARGOT: In 1969 I moved to Ohio and started a new life without my parents.

KENT: One... two... three... four.

MARGOT: Even in their pain I missed them.

RICHARD: When I got to the hospital my mother was standing in the hall.

ANONYMOUS: She disappeared and I never saw her again.

RICHARD: She was dead calm.

ANONYMOUS: I tried to write to her but there was no forwarding address.

RICHARD: She was standing in front of the doors of the intensive care and she was smiling a funny smile I'd never seen before.

ANONYMOUS: I've never seen her again.

RICHARD: I told her I was sorry I was late. She said it didn't matter.

ANONYMOUS: I've always thought I was a good mother.

RICHARD: I asked her where Dad was and she said he was gone.

Nightwalking

ANONYMOUS: Soon I'll be gone and it won't matter where that girl was that day.

RICHARD: I looked at her and asked if she meant he was dead.

ANONYMOUS: Some things have a life of their own.

RICHARD: She said he was dead but that it was all right and I didn't need to cry. She said it was over now and it was all going to be fine.

ANONYMOUS: And that's why I came here today.

RICHARD: She said they had brought all the wounded students into the ward and it was terrible - all the blood and the confusion and the fear. She said you could smell the fear. Even some of the nurses didn't want to touch them. Then one of the doctors came in with the x-rays of the one boy, the one that was shot in the spine, and the doctor was crying he'd never seen a bullet shatter a spine so badly. Mom kept talking about the students and she was smiling now. She said it was all going to be fine. She said the others would all live now.

ANONYMOUS: She must be a woman now... if she's still alive.

KENT: I cried for the kids who died. They were like me. Young.

ANONYMOUS: But she'll always be that young girl to me.

RICHARD: My mother stood there and smiled and said that no one else would die because she had made a pact with God and it really was all over now. She took me in her arms and she smiled because she said the trade had been made - the life had been taken and no more would die. She said it was finally over now and we could go home.

ANONYMOUS: I made her eat to keep her alive but I wouldn't let her take food to those boys. I swear, I'm a good

Voices from Kent State

woman. I paid for every meal I gave her.

RICHARD: She told God that it would be all right to take her husband if the wounded children could live.

KENT: Bang... Bang... Bang...

RICHARD: If only the ones that were wounded wouldn't die...

KENT: Bang.

RICHARD: God could take my father to his eternal resting place.

ANONYMOUS: I've always wondered where she was in the world.

RICHARD: Where he could join his son.

ANONYMOUS: Was she alive? Did she miss me?

RICHARD: And she promised not to mourn either of them anymore.

ANONYMOUS: Did she know what really happened?

RICHARD: Just let them live and she would never say another word.

ANONYMOUS: I never heard another word.

RICHARD: On a warm day in May.

ANONYMOUS: Did she have children?

RICHARD: My mother stopped asking questions.

ANONYMOUS: Did she finish school?

RICHARD: When my father died in a hospital in a little town near where he was born.

ANONYMOUS: Or was there another story I'll never know.

RICHARD: My mother made peace because the children lived.

KENT: One...

ANONYMOUS: I guess there's some things we never know.

KENT: Two...

RICHARD: All the others lived.

KENT: Three.

RICHARD: And we went on and never spoke of it again til now.

Nightwalking

KENT: Four.

ANONYMOUS: But in my mind - she's always kind of frozen in that time.

MARGOT: Some people ask if Sarah knew about the sacrifice and if she ever tried to stop Abraham. Some say Abraham never told her before he went to Mount Moriah and some believe they only spoke of it in passing when he returned. That Abraham told her of the lamb but never spoke of the knife or the binding or the terror in his son's eyes. No one speaks of Isaac. No one writes of how he felt about his father after that day on the mountain. No one writes about the son at all. Some say that Sarah died soon after because of the pain in her heart. Some say Sarah just died because she was old and tired. Some say it was just a test. Some say it was more. Some say that in the end Abraham would never have plunged the knife into his son's flesh. Some say he would. Some say the questions never end to this day and that is the way God wants it.

(Michael and Frank do not speak to one another but out to the audience)

FRANK: I went in and I didn't complain. And I won't complain about the ones who don't fight, but I won't have them shoving it down my throat. Because I don't know what I would have done if I could have got out of that shit hole war and everything else would have turned out the same.

ANONYMOUS: The revolution was coming the boy said, and this time we would get it right.

KENT: Then just a few days later they were shooting on another campus except this time they were all black.

FRANK: Soldiers don't carry empty guns and don't ever forget it.

KENT: And nobody gives a damn about them at all.

MARGOT: In the fall of 1969 I was a newlywed. I took a job teaching high school English, started buying furniture and believed in the power of love. I had never been to a protest or seen a tank. I never thought about the guns being loaded.

FRANK: No matter who's carrying the gun - you be real scared.

GUARDSMAN: We were on lock and load all weekend. People don't understand that. We were told we could fire anytime we felt our lives in danger. People need to know that.

ANONYMOUS: A few minutes before noon I started walking up to the campus.

MICHAEL: We heard the bell ringing on the other side of the hill.

KENT: This was the end of the line.

SHANNON: It was warm and I took my jacket off and laid it down on the ground.

GUARDSMAN: The students started coming. We could see them... fifty... a hundred... a thousand walking towards us.

KENT: This assembly is unlawful... the voice bellowed. The crowd must disperse at this time.

SHANNON: Off the pigs... Off the pigs...

KENT: Fuck the pigs... Fuck the pigs...

RICHARD: One... two... three... four... we don't want your fucking war.

MICHAEL: Two... four... six... eight... we don't want your fascist state.

GUARDSMAN: Disperse, the bull horn blared.

MARGOT: Disperse...

Nightwalking

SHANNON: Disperse...
ANONYMOUS: Disperse...
GUARDSMAN: A rock arched out from the crowd...
ANONYMOUS: Then a brick and a stone...
RICHARD: A few minutes after noon the guard formed a single long line in front of the ruins of the old ROTC building...
MICHAEL: They put on gas masks...
GUARDSMAN: On order they moved out in a skirmish line, bayonets fixed and unsheathed.
MARGOT: Disperse...
SHANNON: Disperse...
ANONYMOUS: Disperse...
MICHAEL: Two...
RICHARD: Four...
KENT: Six...
SHANNON: Eight...
TOGETHER: We don't want your fascist state.
FRANK: You be real scared when you see a gun. Real scared.
MICHAEL: The President had left the campus and no one was in charge.
ANONYMOUS: I tell you it wasn't so innocent up there.
MARGOT: My father died raving at a television and loving Richard Nixon.
ANONYMOUS: I hear that one of the fathers said his daughter's death would always be on that President's head.
MARGOT: Sometimes when I miss my father I think I love Richard Nixon too.
                    (There is a burst of gunfire.)
GUARDSMAN: STOP FIRING!
TOGETHER: Stop firing. *(repeats overlapping like gunfire)*
ANONYMOUS: They say after the shooting started a man in a

uniform ran up and down in front of those boys on the other side.

GUARDSMAN: He hit my gun so hard his stick broke.

KENT: He was yelling "Cease-fire, cease-fire!"

MICHAEL: And it was all over.

ANONYMOUS: I heard the screaming, but I never got further than the front gate.

KENT: I hadn't gone home that day.

RICHARD: My father died but the others lived.

GUARDSMAN: The truckers had stopped when we stood in the doors with our guns. But the students didn't. I wanted to tell them if they came too close we would have to shoot and someone might die - but it was all over before I could speak. I wanted to shout that this was not a test. Sometimes I wake up and my mouth is still open in a scream.

MARGOT: Maybe I wanted to hear the stories so I could make sense of it where the others had failed.

GUARDSMAN: We were lucky because we had these old guns - not the new ones. We were lucky because with the new ones there would have been a massacre.

ANONYMOUS: Sometimes I think about that girl and I can't sleep.

GUARDSMAN: "Don't fire, don't fire" he screamed and when I think about those few moments in my bed at night - our fingers poised, my eyes wet from the gas - my ears ringing from the chants - I am grateful for the old guns. Then I close my eyes and try to sleep.

MARGOT: I wanted to understand it all.

GUARDSMAN: I can't say that my life hasn't been good since then. I have been a happy man.

MARGOT: To have it all fall into place.

GUARDSMAN: I thought someday it would all make sense.

Nightwalking

TOGETHER: Now I'm not so sure.

MARGOT: My father died the day after Nixon resigned. Now Nixon is gone too.

ANONYMOUS: I thought the President of the University would know the truth but he died and never left a word.

FRANK: You don't know everything, son. Believe me, no one does.

GUARDSMAN: I had been on a night patrol on Saturday night when we got into this skirmish near the front gate. Suddenly we were hand-to-hand with some students and before I knew it I had pinned my bayonet into his hand and stopped - just for a moment when we seemed to be looking at one another though his face is as much of a blur now as it was then - then pulling out the bayonet we all ran away into the darkness. I can still feel that moment when the steel went into his hand. I can still remember wiping away the blood with my handkerchief.

KENT: I have a dream about all the dead of that year - They dance around me singing "Don't worry, little brother, the best is yet to come."

GUARDSMAN: I was really happy when they said we'd be leaving that morning. Then they said to unpack and go back to the hill.

ANONYMOUS: I think about that girl and wonder what she thinks about.

RICHARD: I think about my brother and he is a ghost like my father.

ANONYMOUS: Seems wrong to lose your loved ones too young.

SHANNON: I had a fight with Jason and my mother had been giving me hell all night so I came up here for a little peace. I hitchhiked all the way and when I got to the campus I stopped and took off my jacket. It was hot and there were people throwing things and Guardsmen and gas and then suddenly there were shots and screaming and I fell and when I looked up there was this boy bleeding - I had never seen anything die before but you could see it in his eyes. Like the fish my daddy would bring home from the river.

RICHARD: My Dad was dead and none of the others died and I didn't know how to feel.

SHANNON: Gone.

RICHARD: Gone.

MARGOT: Gone.

KENT: Gone.

FRANK: I thought what I did made a difference. Now I just don't know.

RICHARD: When my brother was in Vietnam he used write us letters home every week. He called them his breakfast visits because he would come back from night patrol and write to us before he fell asleep. One of the things that happened to him, he told us, was that he had developed the ability to walk in the dark and see without light. He called it - nightwalking - and he said that somehow, in the middle of all this killing, it had made sense of his life. To nightwalk you needed to forget everything you had been taught. To stop thinking in the same way you had been taught to think - and to stop seeing in the same way you had been taught to see. You needed, he wrote, to "trust the earth in a way no one ever teaches you to - and believe in something that you can't find in churches or schools." He believed that even in the terrible hell that was Vietnam, something greater, something higher

Nightwalking

than what he had come to think of as God... and something more important within the human race than we had yet learned - would come out of all that pain. Those were his words as I remember them. He was sure that the nightwalking would lead him to the truth of his own life... and perhaps the truth of life itself. And when he came home he was going to teach all of us - including his little brother - to do it too. That was the last letter he wrote. He stepped into a rice field mined with bamboo triggers. They said he died before he knew what hit him. But I like to think he had already found what he was looking for. Now on warm nights, when I go walking in the woods near our family home, I feel him, right there beside me, reaching out his hand, taking my hand, now as large as his and we walk together and talk together of all that we have learned, and done and believed. On these nightwalks I am at peace with that day in May and all the other days that have come between my brother and me.

FRANK: It has to make a difference.

KENT: Bang... Bang... Bang...

MARGOT: And the angel called to Abraham a second time and told him that because he had not withheld his son, he would be blessed, his descendants would be made as numerous as the stars of the heaven and as the sand of the seashore. All this, the angel said, "because you have obeyed my command."

ANONYMOUS: They said there were 54 shots fired in 13 seconds.

KENT: It could have been any of us.

ANONYMOUS: If I had just walked a little faster up that hill.

KENT: I think about the space between life and death.

Voices from Kent State

SHANNON: If I hadn't stopped to take off my jacket.
MICHAEL: It could have been me, Dad.
KENT: It could have been me.
GUARDSMAN: If I had just been on the other side of the hill...
MARGOT: Would my husband have died? My daughter never born? My life a different story.
GUARDSMAN: Would I have shot them down?
MARGOT: My daughter never born.
GUARDSMAN: My life a different story.
TOGETHER: Would anyone remember?
MARGOT: I like to think that Sarah would have wanted to stop Abraham. That she wouldn't have let him raise the knife to his son no matter who asked. I like to think that but I'm not really sure.
SHANNON: I had to tell somebody about what happened because it changed my life forever.
ANONYMOUS: I wanted somebody to know that girl saved my life.
SHANNON: I left that day and didn't wake up 'till 1975.
GUARDSMAN: Now I just want it over.
SHANNON: Sometimes I think I'm not awake yet.
MARGOT: I came to hear the stories and I hoped to learn the truth. In the end there are only the stories and the truth must be found by someone else.
CATHERINE: Your father and I love you Michael. Don't we Frank?
KENT: Is it finally over?
MARGOT: My father loved Richard Nixon.
CATHERINE: Tell him you love him Frank. No matter what. Tell him.
MICHAEL: Dad?

(Margot is alone in a spotlight)

Nightwalking

MARGOT: In our life there are markers to help us see how far we have come. Birthdays, anniversaries, awards - to help us look at how well we have passed our time here and how much there is still to do. Sometimes the markers are there for all of us to see. A war won or lost... a revolution failed or still ongoing... a millennium about to change hands. Sometimes they are much more private - a prayer for our dead parent... a graduation for a dear child... an anniversary with a beloved mate. (*Pause*) When I was born my father paid double because he wanted me so badly, but he would die without knowing much about me at all except that he loved me and that has had to be enough. If we are not vigilant, this life will come and go and we will miss it and leave it behind without a trace. If we are not vigilant, we can become bitter or lost or worse. If we are not vigilant, we will mistake the markers for the meaning, and fail the test completely.

BLACKOUT

END OF PLAY

U

KENT STATE UNIVERSITY
KENT, OHIO 44240

OFFICE OF THE PRESIDENT
(216) 672-2210

May 6, 1970

Dear K.S.U. Parents:

Nowhere in the world is the shock of the Kent State campus tragedy more fully felt and more deeply regretted than within our University community. Evidence of the horrors of the violence and disorder are clearly visible. Less visible, but much deeper, are the feelings of personal loss and sympathy for parents of those students who died.

I share with my colleagues a sense of frustration never before experienced. Events during those hectic days were quickly taken from our hands. Off-campus security forces assumed command of the University but, alas, they were unable to quell the forces of violence. Our concern for the health and safety of students, faculty and staff clearly mandated the closing of the University.

At this writing our campus is still patrolled by forces of the Ohio National Guard and other state security agencies. I have, however, received word that the Guardsmen are about to be released from campus duty.

The University is calm. But the picture of a campus secured by armed soldiers and absent its young people does not befit an educational institution. We must, therefore, focus our attention on a reopening of the University.

Before reopening, however, we must and will provide assurances for the safety of those within our charge. We seek normalcy and ask your assistance in reaching that goal. The mechanism for change must be reason - not violence!

Efforts to secure the cooperation of the leadership within faculty and student organizations are underway. We are also working closely with the various security agencies. As soon as definite word on reopening is available you will have immediate notification.

Your understanding, support and assistance and that of your son or daughter on campus is vital to our efforts for reopening. We sincerely hope for your cooperation.

Sincerely,

Robert I. White,
President

Digital reproduction of the original letter.

LETTER

The appearance of armed troops on the campus of Kent State University is an appalling sight. Occupation of the town and campus by National Guardsman is testimony to the domination of irrationality in the policies of our government.
The President of the United States commits an illegal act of war and refers to his opposition as "bums." That students and faculty and, indeed, all thinking people reject his position is not only rational but patriotic. True, burning a building at Kent State University is no joke; we reject such tactics. Yet the burning of an ROTC building is no accident. We deplore this violence but we feel it must be viewed in the larger context of the daily burning of buildings and people by our government in Viet Nam, Laos and now Cambodia.
Leadership must set the example if it is to persuade. There is only one course to follow if the people of this country young and old are to be convinced of the good faith of their leaders: The war must stop. The vendetta against the Black Panthers must stop. The Constitutional rights of all must be defended against any challenge, even from the Department of Justice itself. If Mr. Nixon instead continues his bankrupt, illegal course, the Congress must be called upon to impeach him.
Here and now we repudiate the inflammatory inaccuracies expressed by Governor Rhodes in his press conference today. We urge him to remove the troops from our campus. No problem can be solved as long as the campus is under martial law.
We call upon public authorities to use their high offices to bring about greater understanding of the issues involved in and contributing to the burning of the ROTC building at Kent State University on Saturday, rather than to exploit this incident in a manner that can only inflame the public and increase the confusion among the members of the University community.

Signed by 23 concerned faculty
Kent State University
Sunday Afternoon, May 3, 1970

Transcribed from the original letter

Ohio Governor James A. Rhodes Speech on
Campus Disorders in Kent
May 3, 1970

Now you know everybody here. This is- Robert Kopansky is the District Attorney for the Federal Government. You know the Mayor, Del Corso, Karamonte and Don Kane.

I want to sum this up and then you can ask questions of any of us. We have seen here at the City of Kent, especially, probably the most vicious form of campus oriented violence yet perpetrated by dissident groups and their allies in the State of Ohio for this reason. Most of the dissident groups have operated within the campus. This has moved over where they have threatened and intimidated merchants and people of this community. Now it ceases to be a problem of the Colleges in Ohio. This, now, is the problem of the State of Ohio and I want to assure you that we're going to employ every force of law that we have under our authority not only to get to the bottom of the situation here at Kent- on the campus- in the city- and we have asked the complete cooperation of the District Attorney of the Federal Government because federal supplies were burned and destroyed in the ROTC building and these people, after we can find them- after a complete investigation- will be turned over to the Federal Government.

We have asked the County Prosecutor for a complete and comprehensive investigation. And there are some people now out on probation that- there has been a strong word to the fact that they have participated in this. Now we're going to put a stop to this for this reason. The same group that we're dealing with here today- and there are three or four of them- they only have one thing in mind and that is to destroy higher education in Ohio. And if they continue this and continue what they're doing, they're going to reach their goal for the simple reason that you cannot continue to set fires to buildings that are worth $5 and $10 million dollars because you cannot get replacements from the Ohio General Assembly. And last night I think that we have seen all forms of violence- the worst. And when they start taking over communities, this is when we're going to drive them out of Kent. We're going to make two recommendations to the Ohio General Assembly. Now we've had this at Miami in Oxford, Ohio. Also at Ohio State University and we had 32 police officers injured- and a couple very severe. We have the same groups going from one campus to the other and they use a university- state supported by the tax payers of Ohio as a sanctuary- and in this they make definite plans of burning, destroying, and throwing rocks at police and at the National Guard and the Highway Patrol. We're asking the Legislature that any person throwing a rock, brick or stone at a law enforcement agency of Ohio- a sheriff, policeman, highway patrolman or national guardsman becomes a felony and, secondly, we're going to ask for legislation that any person in the administrative side or as a student- if these people are convicted whether it is a misdemeanor of a felony for participating in a riot. they're automatically dismissed- there is no hearing, no recourse and they cannot enter another State University in the State of Ohio. We are going to eradicate the problem- we're not going to treat the symptoms. And as long as this continues, higher education in Ohio is in jeopardy and if they continue to give permissive consent, they will destroy higher education in this state.

I would like for- we were very fortunate last night we had 700 -- 700 National Guardsmen in this area on the truckers strike. Had they not been here there would have been 14 or 15 other burn- outs and I'm talking about buildings. And it was just through the good fortune of the other incident happening parallel with this one. And that we had here the County Prosecutor, the Mayor, the Chief of Police and the Fire Chief of every law enforcement agency here have been very cohesive in this and I want to congratulate all of them. They've done a great job- everybody here- the City Attorney- everybody here- the Judicial System, all of them have done a good job here but they're limited. There has to be some way of getting some subsidy for these people to fight and these people just move from one campus to the other and terrorize a community. They're worse than the "Brown Shirt" and the communist element and also the "night riders" in the Vigilantes. They're the worst type of people that we harbor in America. And I want to say that they're not going to take over the campus. And the campus now is going to be part of the County and the State of Ohio. There is no sanctuary for these people to burn buildings down of private citizens'- of businesses in a community and then run into a sanctuary. It's over with in Ohio.

Transcribed from the original audio recording.

Other Available Plays by the Author

And the Evening and the Morning Were the First Day
Anna Comnena*
Blue Moon
Cliff Diving*
Covers
Dear Mother and All*
Looking for Red*
Moving Day
The Woman in the White Jogging Suit
Uniform Love

* full length